# CHRISTOPHER COLUMBUS

Many European ships are sailing south and east around the continent of Africa to get to **China's silk and spices** in the **late 1400s**. An Italian sailor named **Christopher Columbus** has a different idea. He asks the king and queen of **Spain** to pay for ships that will sail west. Is there a shortcut to the riches of China? Will Columbus be lost at sea? Or will he find even more than he dreamed of . . .

1

# HOW DID COLUMBUS LEARN TO SAIL?

ON THE CITY OF **GENOA** IN EUROPE, HUNDREDS OF YEARS AGO:

CHRISTOPHER?! YOU HAVE NOT FINISHED THAT CLOTH I ASKED YOU TO WEAVE??!

ALL YOU DO IS STARE OUT THAT WINDOW AT THE SEA!!

DAD, I AM **GOING** TO SEA.

CHRISTOPHER COLUMBUS IS A TEENAGER WHEN HE LEAVES HIS ITALIAN HOME. IN **1476** HE IS IN A GROUP OF SHIPS ATTACKED BY FRENCH SHIPS.

WELL... I WENT TO SEA...

YOU CAN GO TO LAND BY SWIMMING SIX MILES THAT WAY.

IN **1477** HE IS ON A SHIP THAT SAILS INTO THE NORTH ATLANTIC OCEAN BEYOND ICELAND.

THE NORSEMEN SAY ONE OF THEIR MEN, **LEIF ERIKSSON**, FOUND NEW LAND BY SAILING WEST OF HERE.

THAT'S CRAZY!!

HMMM

EUROPEANS WANT **SILK** AND **SPICES** FROM **CHINA**. THE TURKISH EMPIRE HAS CLOSED LAND ROUTES TO ASIA. SAILORS ARE EXPLORING THE COAST OF AFRICA TO SEE IF THEY CAN GET SHIPS AROUND IT TO SAIL EAST TO ASIA. COLUMBUS HAS THE REVERSE IDEA...

KING FERDINAND AND QUEEN ISABELLA OF **SPAIN**, I CAN FIND YOU A NEW ROUTE TO CHINA'S WEALTH! I WILL SAIL **WEST**!

*next:* SARGASS

# WHERE DID COLUMBUS LAND FIRST?

EARLY MORNING ON OCT. 12, 1492...

LAND!

MY NAME IS COLUMBUS. DO YOU KNOW THE WAY TO OHIO?

NEVERMIND. HOW ABOUT GOLD? SILK? SPICES? CHOPSTICKS??

BOYD 02

COLUMBUS IS ON AN ISLAND IN THE CARIBBEAN. THE PEOPLE HE MEETS ARE OF THE TAINO CULTURE. BUT HE CALLS THEM:

INDIANS!

THESE ARE THE INDIES ISLANDS OFF THE COAST OF **CHINA**, RIGHT??

THEY SMOKE TUBES OF LEAVES CALLED "TOBACOS."

BUT WHERE IS THE GOLD?

LOOK! THEY CALL THIS A "HAMACA!"

WHERE IS THE GOLD?

COLUMBUS! THESE ARE "PAROTS."

WHERE IS THE GOLD?!

AWK! Where is the Gold? A

HE NAMES AN ISLAND "HISPANIOLA." WHILE EXPLORING IT, HE CRASHES THE SANTA MARIA ON A SANDBAR.

WOOD FROM THE WRECK WILL MAKE A NICE FORT. YOU 40 MEN LOOK FOR GOLD HERE WHILE THE OTHER CREWMEN AND I RETURN ON THE NIÑA TO SPAIN FOR SUPPLIES.

AFTER 224 DAYS OF TRAVEL, COLUMBUS RETURNS TO SPAIN A HERO.

ADMIRAL!
ADMIRAL!
ADMIRAL!!

next: CHAIN, CHAIN, CHAI

# WHEN WAS COLUMBUS PUT IN CHAINS?

SPAIN, 1493: THE COURT OF KING FERDINAND AND QUEEN ISABELLA...

COLUMBUS, WHAT WILL YOU DO ON YOUR SECOND TRIP TO "THE NEW WORLD?"

CARIBBEAN

I HAVE A LOT OF ITTY BITTY ISLANDS TO NAME!

WHEN COLUMBUS RETURNS WITH 17 SHIPS TO THE CARIBBEAN, HE FINDS:

Disaster

ALL 40 MEN IN MY FORT... KILLED!

HE STARTS ANOTHER SETTLEMENT CALLED ISABELA. HIS COLONISTS ARN'T THE NICEST.

I'M TIRED OF THIS. GROWING FOOD IS HARD.

LET'S KILL INDIANS FOR THEIR FOOD AND GOLD!

⁂SIGH⁂ GOVERNING IS TOO HARD. I'M GOING TO EXPLORE THE ISLAND OF CUBA. PLEASE PUNISH THE BAD SETTLERS.

GIVE THEM TIME OUTS, COLUMBUS?

NO, TRY HANGING A FEW.

COLUMBUS WORKS SO HARD AT MAPPING CARIBBEAN ISLANDS THAT HE GETS SICK. THE 43-YEAR-OLD IS IN A COMA FOR WEEKS.

Rosebud....

HE SURVIVES AND SAILS BACK TO SPAIN FOR MORE SUPPLIES.

THE KING AND QUEEN SEND SOMEONE ELSE TO RUN THE SPANISH BASE ON HISPANIOLA.

COLUMBUS KILLED SPANISH MEN??! AN OUTRAGE!!

HUH! SPANISH GUYS HAVE KILLED 100,000 OF US "INDIANS" IN THREE YEARS.

DURING COLUMBUS' THIRD TRIP TO THE CARIBBEAN, A SPANISH OFFICIAL ARRESTS HIM AND RETURNS HIM TO SPAIN IN CHAINS.

NOW HE IS JUST "ADMIRAL OF THE MOSQUITOES!!"

NEXT: SHIP WRECK

BOYD '02

# WHEN WAS COLUMBUS SHIPWRECKED?

CHRISTOPHER COLUMBUS IN SPAIN, TAKE FOUR!!

RELEASE THE ADMIRAL!

THANK YOU, QUEEN ISABELLA. MAY I HAVE **ONE** MORE CHANCE TO FIND **CHINA**??

OK, BUT **DON'T** STOP AT OUR BASE AT HISPANIOLA. THEY REALLY DON'T LIKE YOU THERE.

IN MAY **1502**, COLUMBUS TAKES FOUR SHIPS WEST. HE CROSSES THE ATLANTIC OCEAN IN 21 DAYS.

MY "HIGH VOYAGE!"

HE EXPLORES THE EAST COAST OF CENTRAL AMERICA, FAILING TO FIND A WATER PASSAGE.

RATS! NO PANAMA CANAL. BUT THIS LOOKS LIKE A GOOD PLACE TO MINE **GOLD**.

KRUNKLE

ADMIRAL!! SHIPWORMS ATE THROUGH ONE OF OUR SHIPS!

THE WORMS SOON DESTROY A SECOND SHIP.

FASTER! GET TO A SPANISH SETTLEMENT BEFORE WE CRUMBLE!!

THEY REACH JAMAICA BEFORE THEIR SHIPS FALL APART.

SOME SAILORS GO TO GET HELP FROM THE BASE ON HISPANIOLA — 500 MILES AWAY!

MONTHS PASS...

JUST SIT RIGHT BACK AND YOU'LL HEAR A TALE...

QUIET!!

AFTER **A YEAR**, COLUMBUS AND HIS MEN ARE RESCUED.

COLUMBUS DIES IN 1506, WITHOUT THE AMERICAN RICHES HE ALWAYS WANTED.

# JOHN CABOT

After Columbus claims this "**New World**" for Spain, other European nations scramble to get their own flags planted on these shores. An Italian sailor named **John Cabot** tells the **English** king that he may have the quickest path to the new land: through the bitter North Atlantic Ocean. The English king decides to take a chance that Cabot may be right . . .

# WHERE DID CINNAMON COME FROM

UGH!

oh·· OUCH! ARE WE THERE YET?

NO.

BOYD '00

OW OW OWWARE WE THERE YET?

NO.

ARE WE THERE YET?!

YES, **NOW** WE ARE THERE, SAMUEL! WE ARE IN MECCA, A TRADING CITY IN THE MIDEAST. IT IS **1485**, AND WE ARE ABOUT TO DELIVER THE GOODS...

SPICES

THAT'S US!

THANKYOU THANKYOU THANKYOU! THANKYOU! THESE SPICES WILL GET ME A **LOT** IN EUROPE! PEOPLE NEED SPICES TO FLAVOR THEIR ROTTING FOOD!

IN THESE DAYS THERE ARE NO REFRIGERATORS TO KEEP MEAT FRESH!

UNK!

CINNAMON

NUTMEG

CLOVES

GINGER

PEPPER

ASIAN SPICES HAVE BEEN A BIG DEAL IN EUROPE SINCE **MARCO POLO** WENT TO CHINA IN **1271** AND RETURNED WITH STORIES OF GOLD AND SPICES. BUT MOVING SPICES WEST TAKES **MONTHS** OF CAMEL-RIDING!

Travels of Marco Polo

**OUCH**, I KNOW IT HEY, AREN'T WE DELIVERING OUR OTH SPICES TO A GUY W TAKES THEM TO ITAL

**GIOVANNI CABO** AT YOUR SERVICE

*next:* DISCOVER ITA

# WHICH KING BELIEVED JOHN CABOT'

ITALIAN MAPMAKER GIOVANNI CABOTO MOVES HIS FAMILY TO ENGLAND ABOUT **1495**. THEY LIVE IN BRISTOL, A PORT ON THE WEST SIDE OF ENGLAND. AND CABOTO PICKS UP AN ENGLISH NAME...

**JOHN CABOT!** DO YOU HAVE THAT MAP READY

YES, HERE IT IS. I EVEN SKETCHED THAT LAND SOME OF THE FISHERMEN HAVE BEEN WHISPERING ABOUT.

I'VE HEARD THE RUMORS, TOO — BUT OTHER MAPS DO NOT SHOW IT. SOMETHING TO CHECK OUT SOMEDAY, eh?

YES, SOMETHING FOR **ME** TO CHECK OUT — WITH THE HELP OF **ENGLAND'S KING!**

**I**N **LONDON,** THE COURT OF **HENRY VII:**

SIRE, COLUMBUS DID NOT REACH **CHINA,** JUS SOME OF ITS OFFSHOF ISLANDS. WE CAN BE TRULY FIRST!

WE CAN ALSO BE FASTER. THE EARTH IS A **SPHERE,** SO THE DISTANCE FROM ENGLAND TO CHINA IS SHORTER IN THE NORTHERN LATITUDES THAN FROM SPAIN TO CHINA. WE CAN CONTROL THE SPICE TRADE!

MAKE IT SO!

CABOT GETS A SMALL SHIP, THE "MATTHEW." HIS FIRST TRY GOES NOWHERE. IN MAY **1497** CABOT SAILS AGAIN WITH 18 MEN AND HIS SON SEBASTIAN

*next:* NEW FOUND LAN

# WHATEVER HAPPENED TO JOHN CABOT?

ON AUG. 6, 1497, **JOHN CABOT** RETURNS TO ENGLAND...

I DISCOVERED CHINA!

YOU DISCOVERED **FISH!**

IT'S NOT GOLD, BUT WE CAN SELL THAT FISH FOR A **LOT** TO OTHER NATIONS!

**KING HENRY VII**, I WOULD LIKE ANOTHER TRIP TO SAIL FARTHER SOUTH ALONG THE COAST I FOUND.

YOU SHALL HAVE **FIVE** SHIPS THIS TIME! GO! GO! GO!

CABOT SAILS IN MAY **1498** — RIGHT INTO A STORM. ONE OF HIS SHIPS IS SO BADLY DAMAGED THAT IT TURNS BACK TO A PORT IN IRELAND...

NO RECORD EXISTS OF WHAT HAPPENS TO CABOT AFTER THE STORM. DID HE SINK? DID HE MAKE IT TO AMERICA?

THE **SPANISH** THINK CABOT MADE IT DOWN THE COAST OF NORTH AMERICA AS FAR AS MY CHESAPEAKE BAY. A SPANISH MAP IN **1500** SHOWS ENGLISH FLAGS CLAIMING THAT COASTLINE.

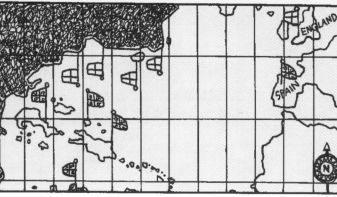

CABOT DID NOT FIND CHINA. BUT HE GAVE ENGLAND CLAIM TO AMERICA AT A TIME WHEN SPAIN CLAIMED MUCH OF THIS "NEW WORLD."

ENGLAND'S CLAIM TOOK HOLD 100 YEARS LATER AT *Jamestown, Va.*

# CHAPTER 3

# THE FRENCH IN CANADA

The **French** quickly follow John Cabot's trail to the northern part of the "New World." Explorers such as **Cartier, Champlain,** and **LaSalle** mark the **Great Lakes region** for France. Will these new settlements be at war with the **American Indians** who already live there? Or will French fur trappers find a way to live and work in peace with these first Americans?

# WHEN DID THE FRENCH SAIL WEST?

The French in North America

SPAIN CONTROLS CENTRAL AND SOUTH AMERICA IN THE 1500s. THIS IS THE STORY OF EXPLORING THE **NORTH.**

JOHN CABOT — AN ITALIAN SEAMAN WITH AN ENGLISH SHIP — SETS FOOT ON NORTH AMERICA IN 1497.

"NEW FOUND LAND!" THIS MUST BE PART OF CHINA! I HAVE FOUND A NEW ROUTE FOR TRADING!

CHINA? THEN WHERE IS THE GREAT WALL?

FRENCH FISHERMEN FOLLOW CABOT'S TRAIL...

LOOK AT ALL THE FISH WE CATCH HERE!

DO YOU THINK NEWFOUNDLAND IS REALLY CHINA?

NAAAH — BUT MAYBE RIVERS NEAR HERE GO **TO** CHINA...

IN 1534, FRENCH KING FRANCIS I SENDS 61 MEN ON A MISSION:

FIND A **NORTHWEST PASSAGE.** CLAIM IT FOR **FRANCE!**

A QUICK SEA LANE TO CHINA WILL GIVE US POWER. SPAIN WON'T GET **ALL** THE GLORY!

THIS MISSION IS LED BY **JACQUES CARTIER.**

CARTIER'S TRAVELS PROVE NEWFOUND-LAND IS AN ISLAND. HE ALSO SAILS

WOAH! WHO ARE YOU?!!

I AM CLEAVE BEAVER. I AM SHOWING THESE PEOPLE THEIR **FIRST EUROPEANS** YOU'RE NOT THE ONLY EDUCATIONAL ANIMAL, Y'KNOW.

BOYD '00

next: BUCKTOOTH TALES

# WHAT DID CARTIER DISCOV--ah, RENAME?

CARTIER 1535-36

HOCHELAGA MOUNT ROYAL

ST. LAWRENCE RIVER

NEWFOUNDLAND

Atlantic Ocean

*The French in North America*

CHESTER AND CLEVE BEAVER ARE TRACING HOW THE FRENCH EXPLORED NORTH AMERICA AND ITS PEOPLE.

FRENCHMEN SUCH AS JACQUES CARTIER CALL THIS **"THE NEW WORLD."** HE DISCOVERS—

**DISCOVERS?!** AS IF NOBODY LIVES HERE?! "INDIANS" HAVE LIVED HERE FOR CENTURIES!

SADLY, THE EUROPEANS WILL REALLY CHANGE LIFE FOR NORTH AMERICA'S PEOPLE.

AT LEAST CARTIER **BARTERS** (TRADES) WITH THEM AS EQUALS. HE TREATS INDIANS BETTER THAN THE SPANISH DO — THEY **ENSLAVE THEM** DOWN IN THE CARIBBEAN.

DONNACONNA, I MUST FIND A WATERWAY TO CHINA — A **"NORTHWEST PASSAGE!"**

YOU WILL FREEZE! ICE DEVILS WILL TAKE YOUR SHIP! **DON'T GO!!**

IN 1535 CARTIER DOES GO. HE DISCOVERS

AHEM!

AH, HE... **NOTICES** A LARGE RIVER. WE NOW CALL IT THE SAINT LAWRENCE RIVER. HE SAILS UP THAT RIVER TO AN INDIAN TOWN CALLED HOCHELAGA.

I NAME THIS HILL **"MOUNT ROYAL!"** BUT THAT'S ALL MY NAMING FOR NOW. THOSE RIVER RAPIDS STOP ME FROM SAILING FARTHER INLAND THIS YEAR.

*next:* QUEBEC AND FORTH

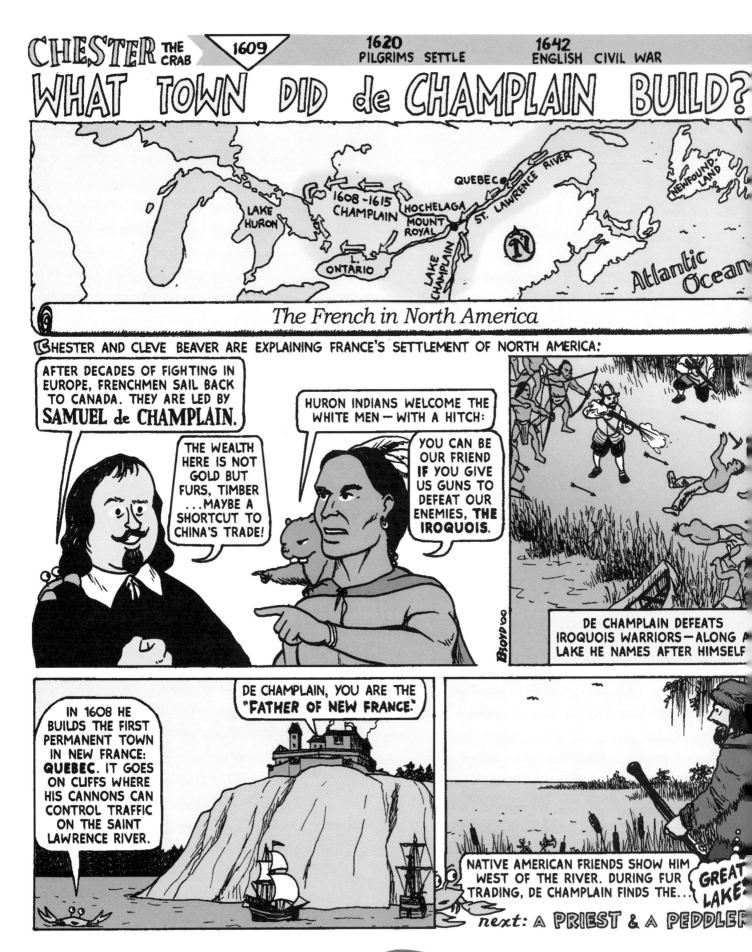

# WHAT TOWN DID de CHAMPLAIN BUILD?

*The French in North America*

CHESTER AND CLEVE BEAVER ARE EXPLAINING FRANCE'S SETTLEMENT OF NORTH AMERICA:

AFTER DECADES OF FIGHTING IN EUROPE, FRENCHMEN SAIL BACK TO CANADA. THEY ARE LED BY **SAMUEL de CHAMPLAIN.**

THE WEALTH HERE IS NOT GOLD BUT FURS, TIMBER ...MAYBE A SHORTCUT TO CHINA'S TRADE!

HURON INDIANS WELCOME THE WHITE MEN — WITH A HITCH:

YOU CAN BE OUR FRIEND **IF** YOU GIVE US GUNS TO DEFEAT OUR ENEMIES, **THE IROQUOIS.**

DE CHAMPLAIN DEFEATS IROQUOIS WARRIORS — ALONG A LAKE HE NAMES AFTER HIMSELF

IN 1608 HE BUILDS THE FIRST PERMANENT TOWN IN NEW FRANCE: **QUEBEC.** IT GOES ON CLIFFS WHERE HIS CANNONS CAN CONTROL TRAFFIC ON THE SAINT LAWRENCE RIVER.

DE CHAMPLAIN, YOU ARE THE "FATHER OF NEW FRANCE."

NATIVE AMERICAN FRIENDS SHOW HIM WEST OF THE RIVER. DURING FUR TRADING, DE CHAMPLAIN FINDS THE... GREAT LAKES

*next:* A PRIEST & A PEDDLER

# WHO PADDLED THE MISSISSIPPI RIVER?

**Map labels:** LAKE SUPERIOR · LAKE MICHIGAN · LAKE HURON · L. ONTARIO · LAKE ERIE · QUEBEC · MONTREAL · ST. LAWRENCE RIVER · FORT CROWN POINT · LAKE CHAMPLAIN · Atlantic Ocean · ILLINOIS RIVER · 1673 MARQUETTE AND JOLLIET RIVER · MISSISSIPPI · BRITISH · SPANISH · Gulf of Mexico

BY THE 1600s THOSE WACKY FRENCH HAVE A BIG TRADING NETWORK WITH AMERICAN INDIANS. THEY GET VALUABLE **FURS** FROM POOR ANIMALS LIKE **ME**, CLEVE BEAVER. BUT ARE THEY HAPPY WITH THAT?! **NOOOOOOO!!**

IN **1672** FRANCE SENDS TRADER **LOUIS JOLLIET** TO FIND A RIVER TO THE **PACIFIC OCEAN**...

WHAT DO YOU THINK, **JACQUES MARQUETTE?**

THE INDIANS I PREACH TO TALK OF A "GREAT RIVER" SOUTH OF LAKE MICHIGAN.

TWO INDIANS GUIDE THE FRENCHMEN UP THE FOX RIVER IN 1673. THEY CARRY THEIR SUPPLIES A FEW MILES OVER LAND AND FIND:

FATHER MARQUETTE! THIS WATER DOESN'T FLOW EAST TO QUEBEC — IT FLOWS **SOUTH!!**

FURRY HORSIES!

BISON.

THEY RIDE THE WISCONSIN RIVER UNTIL IT JOINS THE MISSISSIPPI — LONGEST RIVER IN NORTH AMERICA.

THESE MEN MAP 1000 MILES OF THE RIVER. ANGRY INDIANS FINALLY MAKE JOLLIET AND MARQUETTE STOP.

**REVERSE!!**

THEY DO NOT FIND A WATERWAY TO CHINA. BUT THIS TEAM GIVES FRANCE A CLAIM TO ONE OF AMERICA'S RICHEST **NATURAL RESOURCES!**

*next: La Salle*

# WHAT LAND DID La SALLE CLAIM?

THE FRENCH ARE MAD THAT THE SPANISH CONTROL WHERE THE MISSISSIPPI RIVER MEETS THE GULF OF MEXICO.

WE NEED A MAN TO FINISH WHAT JOLLIET CLAIMED ON HIS TRIP ON THE MISSISSIPPI.

BATMAN!

THE ROCK!

René-Robert Cavelier Sieur de LaSalle!

LA SALLE GOES SOUTH ON THE MISSISSIPPI, NORTH AMERICA'S LONGEST RIVER.

HIS TEAM BUILDS FORTS TO GUARD FRANCE'S CLAIM TO THE LAND.

IN APRIL 1682 LA SALLE REACHES THE MOUTH OF THE MISSISSIPPI.

I AM THE FIRST WHITE GUY TO TRAVEL THE WHOLE MISSISSIPPI RIVER!!

LA SALLE RETURNS IN 1684 WITH 320 SETTLERS. THIS TIME HE COMES FROM THE GULF OF MEXICO END — AND HE CANNOT FIND THE MISSISSIPPI!

THE SETTLERS REBEL AND KILL LA SALLE.

OUR TRIBE HAS VOTED YOU OFF!

STILL, LA SALLE HAS MARKED THIS TERRITORY FOR FRANCE AND KING LOUIS XIV. THE UNITED STATES BUYS THIS LAND FROM FRANCE IN 1803. END

18

# CHAPTER 4

# THE SPANISH IN FLORIDA

Meanwhile, the **Spanish** tighten their grip on the southern regions of the Americas. Their continuing search for **gold** leads Spanish explorer **Juan Ponce DeLeon** to a land of flowers. He names it "**Florida**" and claims it for Spain. DeLeon also hears a rumor that Florida has a fountain of water that can keep someone young forever . . .

# WHO WAS JUAN PONCE de LEÓN?

CHESTER, WHERE ARE WE? AND WHAT IS THAT... SWEET SMELL?

THIS IS THE CARIBBEAN ISLAND OF HISPANIOLA. WE ARE ON A SUGAR CANE PLANTATION WITH **JUAN PONCE de LEÓN.** HE IS ONE OF THE SPANISH EXPLORERS WHO CONQUERED THIS LAND.

YOU TELLING THE TRUTH, SLAVE?!

YES! YES! THERE IS... **MUCH** GOLD ON ANOTHER ISLAND! GO TO BORINQUEN!

IN 1508 DE LEÓN EXPLORES BORINQUEN. HE FINDS SOME GOLD.

HMMMM. WE HAVEN'T FOUND MUCH GOLD ON THESE ISLANDS SINCE COLUMBUS LANDED HERE IN 1492. BUT MAYBE BORINQUEN WILL BE GOLDEN...

YOU THINK **THIS** IS GREAT? YOU SHOULD SEE THE FOUNTAIN OF YOUTH ON BIMINI!

IT SOUNDS LIKE THESE GUYS JUST WANT HIM TO GO SOMEWHERE **ELSE.**

IN MARCH 1513 DE LEON TAKES THREE SHIPS OUT FROM BORINQUEN (PUERTO RICO).

I AM IN MY 50s NOW. IF I FIND THIS SPRING OF WATER THE INDIANS TALK ABOUT, I CAN BE YOUNG **AND** RICH!

MAYBE HE WILL DISCOVER BEVERLY HILLS 90210?

BOYD '00

FIRST HE MUST GET PAST SOME OBSTACLES. THE SPANIS HAVE NO MAPS SHOWING LAND NORTH OF THE CARIBBEA SEA. THREE WEEKS INTO HIS TRIP, **A STORM HITS!**

next: *LAND of FLOWERS*

# HOW DID FLORIDA TREAT de LEÓN?

AFTER SAILING UNMAPPED WATERS FOR WEEKS, SPANISH SOLDIER **JUAN PONCE DE LEÓN** HITS SHORE IN **1513.**

THIS BEACH IS PRETTY! NAME IT "LA FLORIDA"— BASED ON THE SPANISH WORD FOR FLOWER.

DE LEÓN IS THE FIRST EUROPEAN TO WALK IN WHAT WILL BE THE UNITED STATES.

HE SAILS ALONG FLORIDA'S EAST COAST. THE FIRST INDIANS HE FINDS ATTACK HIS BOAT GOING ASHORE.

MAYBE THEY HEARD HOW WE'VE MADE INDIANS OUR SLAVES!?

THE FLEET SAILS UP FLORIDA'S WEST COAST. ONE DAY INDIANS ROW OUT, ASKING TO TRADE. **THEN THEY ATTACK!!**

OK! WHO WANTS TO GO BACK TO PUERTO RICO?

ME! ME! ME

BACK IN PUERTO RICO, DE LEON PLANS ANOTHER TRIP. IN 1521 HE RETURNS TO FLORIDA AND IS IMMEDIATELY ATTACKED BY INDIANS ON THE BEACH.

WHEN WILL WE GET THE MESSAGE?

DE LEÓN IS HIT WITH AN ARROW. THE SPANISH SAIL AWAY, AND HE DIES A FEW WEEKS LATER IN CUBA.

THAT WAS A SHORT EPISODE, CHESTER.

IT'S NOT OVER YET!

THE SPANISH WILL NOT GIVE UP THEIR SEARCH FOR GOLD. IN 1539 **HERNANDO de SOTO** LEADS SOLDIERS INTO FLORIDA'S SWAMPS. HE FINDS NO GOLD—ONLY MORE ANGRY INDIANS.

IN 1564...

**KING PHILLIP II!** FRANCE JUST BUILT A FORT IN FLORIDA. THEY ARE SQUEEZING YOUR CLAIMS!

GET ME DON PEDRO MENENDEZ DE AVILES! **HE** WILL CONQUER FLORIDA FOR ME!

*next:* **ST. AUGUSTINE**

# WHEN WAS ST. AUGUSTINE SETTLED?

HERE WE GO AGAIN.

IN **1565** SPANISH SOLDIERS LAND IN FLORIDA, WHERE EXPLORER JUAN PONCE DE LEÓN LANDED 50 YEARS BEFORE. THE'RE LED BY **Don Pedro Menéndez de Avilés.**

WE CLAIM THIS SAND! OUR FIRST MISSION: DESTROY FRANCE'S FORT CAROLINE NEARBY!

OFFICIAL SPANISH FLAG-PLANTING SPOT

MENÉNDEZ DESTROYS FRANCE'S OUTPOST AND BUILDS HIS OWN: **ST. AUGUSTINE.**

FROM HERE WE CAN SEE ANY SHIPS USING THE GULF STREAM TO SAIL THE ATLANTIC OCEAN

IT IS AN IMPORTANT SPOT. IN **1586** ENGLISH EXPLORER **Sir FRANCIS DRAKE** ATTACKS!

THIS SAND WILL BELONG TO **ENGLAND** AFTER WE BURN THAT SILLY LOG FORT TO THE GROUND!

BOYD '00

DID THAT DEFEAT MAKE THE SPANISH FINALLY LEAVE FLORIDA?

NO WAY!

WE NEED A **STONE** FORT. MAYBE THIS COQUINA FROM THE HARBOR WILL WORK?

THE SPANISH SPEND YEARS MAKING CASTILLO DE SAN MARCOS IN ST. AUGUSTINE.

MEANWHILE, ENGLISHMEN BUILD A COLONY CALLED VIRGINIA NORTH OF FLORIDA.

IN 1702 THE ENGLISH ATTACK ST. AUGUSTINE AGAIN. **THIS TIME** THEIR CANNONBALLS BOUNCE OFF THE POROUS WALLS MADE OF PACKED SHELLS.

Boing.

THE 1,200 PEOPLE OF ST. AUGUSTINE STAY SAFE INSIDE THE FORT WALLS FOR TWO MONTHS. SPANISH SHIPS FINALLY ARRIVE TO DRIVE OFF THE ENGLISH.

OUCH!

next **FLIGHT AND FIGHT**

# WHO BUILT FLORIDA'S FORT MOSÉ?

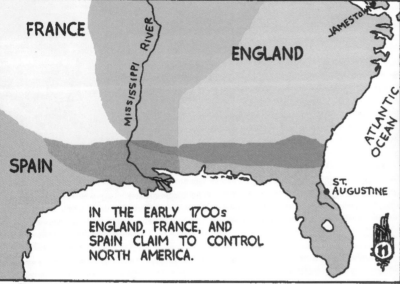

IN THE EARLY 1700s ENGLAND, FRANCE, AND SPAIN CLAIM TO CONTROL NORTH AMERICA.

TO WEAKEN THE BRITISH COLONIES, THE SPANISH IN FLORIDA PROMISE FREEDOM TO ANY SLAVE ESCAPING BRITAIN'S **GEORGIA** OR **CAROLINA** COLONIES. MANY SLAVES SNEAK THROUGH ALLIGATOR-PACKED SWAMPS TO REACH SPAIN'S ST. AUGUSTINE, FLORIDA.

**NO**, WE DIDN'T MEAN YOU COULD LIVE WITH US — GO BUILD YOUR **OWN** TOWN!

IN 1738 THE EX-SLAVES BUILD **FORT MOSÉ**, JUST NORTH OF ST. AUGUSTINE.

TWO YEARS LATER ENGLISHMAN *James Oglethorpe* LEADS GEORGIA COLONISTS AGAINST FORT MOSÉ. OGLETHORPE IS BEATEN BACK. THEN THE **FRENCH AND INDIAN WAR** BEGINS (TO SEE WHICH NATION WILL CONTROL NORTH AMERICA).

THE WINNER: **BRITAIN!** A TREATY ENDING THE WAR IN **1763** GIVES FLORIDA TO BRITAIN. THE PEOPLE OF FORT MOSÉ LEAVE...

WE WILL GO TO CUBA RATHER THAN RETURN TO BRITISH PLANTATIONS.

FLORIDA IS QUIET — FOR A FEW MONTHS. THEN THE **AMERICAN REVOLUTION** BEGINS! SPAIN SEES ITS CHANCE TO RECLAIM FLORIDA. SPAIN SENDS MONEY TO HELP AMERICAN COLONISTS DEFEAT BRITAIN.

SURE ENOUGH, WHEN THE BRITISH COLONIES WIN THEIR INDEPENDENCE, SPAIN GETS FLORIDA BACK IN **1783'S** "TREATY OF PARIS."

*next:* SEMINOLE WORK

23

# WHEN DID FLORIDA JOIN THE U.S.?

WHEN THE SPANISH SETTLED ST. AUGUSTINE, FLORIDA, IN 1565, THEY MET TIMUCUAS INDIANS. SPANISH DISEASES KILLED THE WHOLE TRIBE. IN THE LATE 1700s, DIFFERENT INDIANS COME.

¡HASTA LUEGO CIMARRÓNES!

TO ENGLISH EARS, THAT SOUNDS LIKE "SEM-AH-NOLES." THE SPANISH WORD MEANS "PEOPLE WHO LOVE FREEDOM."

THE SEMINOLES COME FROM CREEK INDIAN TRIBES IN THE AMERICAN SOUTHEAST. WHITE SETTLERS PUSH THEM AWAY FROM THEIR HOMELANDS

UNITED STATES GENERAL **ANDREW JACKSON** CROSSES HIS ARMY INTO SPANISH LAND IN **1818**. HE SAYS HE IS LOOKING FOR RUNAWAY SLAVES — BUT HE USES THIS INVASION TO ATTACK SEMINOLES.

Gulp! CRAZY JACKSON PROVES THE U.S. IS HUNGRY FOR OUR LAND.

WE SHOULD JUST SELL FLORIDA TO THE U.S. RATHER THAN FIGHT MORE.

FOR SALE

FLORIDA BECOMES A U.S. TERRITORY IN **1821**. GUESS WHO BECOMES FLORIDA'S GOVERNOR?!

OK, ALL SEMINOLES GET OUT!

A MAN NAMED **OSCEOLA** LEADS SEMINOLE WARRIORS TO ATTACK U.S. TROOPS. HE IS CAPTURED, AND SEMINOLES ARE FORCED TO MOVE WEST. SOME STAY HIDDEN IN FLORIDA'S SWAMPS

FLORIDA BECOMES THE 27TH U.S. STATE IN **1845**. SEMINOLE INDIANS LIVE THERE TODAY, AND ST. AUGUSTINE STILL STANDS AS THE **OLDEST EUROPEAN SETTLEMENT IN THE UNITED STATES!** END

SINCE 1565